The Casting Of Bells

Other Titles From The Spirit That Moves Us Press

*Editor's Choice: Literature & Graphics from the U. S. Small Press,
1965-1977*

Nuke-Rebuke: Writers & Artists Against Nuclear Energy & Weapons

The Spirit That Moves Us Reader: Seventh Anniversary Anthology

The Farm In Calabria & Other Poems, by David Ray

The Actualist Anthology

The Poem You Asked For, by Marianne Wolfe

Cross-Fertilization: The Human Spirit As Place

Riverside, by Morty Sklar

Forthcoming:

Here's The Story: Contemporary Fiction With A Heart (winter 1983)

*Editor's Choice II: Poetry & Fiction from the U. S. Small Press,
1978-1983* (1984)

Ongoing: *The Spirit That Moves Us* magazine, since 1975

For our complete catalog, write to The Spirit That Moves Us Press,
P. O. Box 1585, Iowa City, Iowa 52244

Jaroslav Seifert

THE CASTING OF BELLS

Translated from the Czech by
Paul Jagasich & Tom O'Grady

No. 4 of the Outstanding Author Series
This book is also offered to subscribers to
The Spirit That Moves Us as part
of their subscriptions.

The Spirit That Moves Us Press : Iowa City

Acknowledgements

Some of these translations previously appeared in *The Hampden-Sydney Poetry Review* and *An Anthology of Modern Magazine Verse*. The publisher wishes to express his gratitude to Hampden-Sydney College for its purchase of copies of this book in support of its publication.

The translators wish to acknowledge a grant from Hampden-Sydney College, thru which much of the translation of this collection was made.

Cover design & execution by Richard McClintock

2nd printing, with revised Foreword, November 1984
3,000 trade paperbacks & 1,000 clothbound

The first printing (First U.S. Edition) was published August 1983,
and limited to 1,000 trade paperbacks

Manufactured in the U.S.A. by McNaughton & Gunn

Library of Congress Cataloging in Publication Data:

Seifert, Jaroslav, 1901-
The casting of bells.

(Outstanding author series ; no. 4)
Translation of: Odlevani zvonu.
"Some of these translations previously appeared in The Hampden-Sydney Poetry Review and in An Anthology of Modern Magazine Verse"–T.p. verso
I. Jagasich, Paul. II. O'Grady, Tom, 1943-
III. Title. IV. Series
PG5038.S450313 1983   891.8'615   83-10631
ISBN 0-930370-25-2
ISBN 0-930370-26-0 (pbk.)

Foreword

Jaroslav Seifert was born in Prague, Czechoslovakia in 1901. He worked for years as a journalist and a translator of French and Russian manuscripts. The Author of more than twenty books of poetry, he published his first volume, *A City In Tears*, in 1921. *The Casting Of Bells*, his latest collection, first appeared in Prague in 1967. A selection of his poems, *She Is Loneliest When Mad*, was published in 1968.

In June 1969, Jaroslav Seifert was elected chairman of the Czech Writers Union, even though his books had been suppressed as the result of his activities encouraging free speech during the ill-fated "Prague Spring" of 1968.

We were first introduced to the poetry of Jaroslav Seifert in 1978 when his name came up during a conversation with an editor at *New Yorker* magazine. It was pointed out that Seifert was indeed an important European poet whose work was not widely translated into English. A week later, a copy of *The Casting Of Bells* appeared in the mail. We were intrigued but dismayed. This poet is so accessible yet so subtle; easy yet complex. His range of mind and whimsy overwhelmed us, but we tried to bring a few short poems to English. They seemed to sound close. But the longer, more involved poetry lay ahead. We were trying pieces, not the book: sections, flourishes, not the total scope of this man's art. And yet, as the months went by, the whole body was gradually brought into an English version. We could then stand back and admire how skillfully this entire work was built. *The Casting Of Bells* is a single interconnected statement. Our rendering is a mere attempt to capture some of its grace. Anyone who dares to stand between a poet and his language must do so out of love, out of a humble desire to have other people celebrate the poet's craft. What is offered here is a rendering into English of a rich sensibility, not an exact and finished poetry. This translation is an introduction to the poetry of Jaroslav Seifert. We tried to stay as close as possible to the original. We encourage others to continue with his work, to better shape it, to hone it, someday, into that real, precise voice living in another world.

Paul Jagasich and *Tom O'Grady*
Hampden-Sydney, Virginia
Summer 1981

5

About The Translators

Paul Anthony Jagasich. A native of Hungary, he finished his Slavic and Romance language studies at The University of North Carolina, Chapel Hill, where he received his Ph.D. in 1973. He has lectured and published articles on "Why Romanian Should Be Considered a Major Romance Tongue," "Magyar Lexical Borrowings in Romanian," and "On the Polish Future Tense Systems." He translated "On the Skitrack" from the Russian for *The Literary Review*, and translated from the Czech for *The Hampden-Sydney Poetry Review*. He is in the process of publishing his dictionary of "Non-Finno-Ugrian Linguistic Elements in Hungarian Non-Indoeuropean)" through Xerox-International.

Tom O'Grady. Born in Baltimore in 1943. He studied at The University of Baltimore, Johns Hopkins University and the University of Delaware, and has taught at colleges in Maryland, Delaware and Virginia. His poems and essays have appeared in a variety of magazines throughout the country, and he has two books of his own poetry: *The Farmville Elegies* and *Establishing A Vineyard: A Sonnet Sequence*. Presently a member of the English faculty at Hampden-Sydney College, he is co-founder and editor of *The Hampden-Sydney Poetry Review*, works regularly in the Virginia Poets-in-th-Schools program, and is the proprietor of the Rose Bower Vineyard and Winery.

CONTENTS

7

PROLOGUE

Being a poet is not quite so.

The lark appears in the forest
Flying over the nest
And cannot stop thinking
—Oh, you sinful bliss:
Warm, tossed-up mold
Under my lover's arm.

A dove goes through those same woods
Because she hears voices,
And all gently quivers around her.
I am now watching
A group of young women—
One there; another:
Those that disappear quietly
And evoke only yearning.
No,
I am only leaves and blossoms,
And the rose-colored flowers of trees
Which sparkle after a rain:
So beautiful in the daylight,
But then, at night . . .
But I cannot be this.

When a poet raised his voice
And blood gushed forth,
Men rushed to their weapons
And women started madly cutting
Their dark and golden hair
For bowstrings.
Clean strands, stronger than nylon cord.
Now they all have short hair
And hurry to the injured

And carefully place antiseptic bandages
Upon human wounds
And put our bleeding heads
On a stretcher's white pillow—
They do the least to us.

If the tyrant does not fall
(and even that we inherit)
The poet is sentenced to silence
And the clenched fist opens
To spread over the singer's mouth.
But he shouts his verses through bars,
While book thieves
Get to work fast,
       But I am not him.

Sometimes doubt beats one word against another
To forge certainty,
But it is never the one truth in this world.
And heated words walk limp
A brief distance, until death,
Where they remain an unspoken secret
Setting fire to a darkness that does not move
In the enormous grave
But only clings
To miserable bones:
The mark of fire
Which they left in the pocket
Of the shot victim.
       But I am not him.

"I DON'T LOOK AT PEOPLE'S SOULS."

I don't look at people's souls.
I say to myself, "We'll see."
    But the sounds make us hurry.
They keep repeating: love, love,
As if today there were nothing else.
Many a time I admit my verses
Were flying from illuminated ceilings,
And became dancing letters—
Even when shootings started in the streets again.

She who had so often
Danced on Labut Lake
Has gotten frozen toes
And suffers.

"IT WAS AFTERNOON OR LATER,"

It was afternoon or later,
A meal under the oak,
Difficult to remember.
The maid happily spread the wash in the yard
Shaking each piece with both round hands
And as if this had defied the flat sky above
A rain, as short and ridiculous
As a child's piano with twelve keys,
Began to cool the air.
The clothes hung limp and would not dry.
And from behind the river's mist
The round white moon rose suddenly.

Someone must have noticed
When she swam in Machov Lake
The floating shirts impatiently against her . . .
Of that I could sing,
But not now.

"POOR MOON, SHE IS HELPLESS."

Poor moon, she is helpless.
We are there already, at home.
Already the diggers' shovels fall
and out pours David's silvery tones.
Already fine grass is sown
in the groins of volcanoes.

And where to now?

Don't crowd the emergency exits.
Moons watch women
        and women watch the moon.
They are ruled from white sky.
No, it's not shocking,
        but something embraces you.
This is an ancient curve of life,
of love and blood.

Not long ago women were still working with the loom
and wove sheets
        for their wedding bed
and shared their secrets with the moon.

"I REMAINED ON THIS EARTH"

I remained on this earth
to be your buttercup, Mary.
They are more shy than a lamb's hoof
and are afraid of every storm.

When I feel like sleeping
The grass can shut my eyes.
And to you up there,
      good-bye, good-bye.

Soft, soothing rain washes the light from your face.
And awakening will be beautiful tomorrow
Lying under a sky
Black as a coffin.

"I JUST WANTED TO TELL YOU THIS."

I just wanted to tell you this.
Now you can have a restless night.

Ragged, scattered clouds
like notebook pages hastily put together
pass through the lenses of a telescope.
Each hazy cloud
which has long been lumped together with the stars,
makes its small circle in the blackness
but you have nothing left.
What could you have selected from that pattern?

Nothing. Absolutely nothing. Just poetry.

SHIP IN FLAMES

I was preparing for the night.
Whoever seeks
   will be expected.
Whoever is waiting
   will be found.

I was looking for a place where I could sleep,
concealed somewhere behind the evergreens
where there was a bit of music
left from the spring,
and I could let the night fall upon me.

Flames pierced the darkness and
Someone cried out:
   The ship is burning!
Passionate flames
rose above the pale flat waters
and my lover's arms
   lingered with need.

Under the nervous branches of willow trees
shade covers the well,
fog lies thick over the bottom.
In daylight,
   I could look at my lover.
When the light moved the dark sky away
She came trembling from the well
with the wet bucket.

I dared not ask
if she had seen the flames.
She looked at me surprised,
turned her head
and, after a moment, she nodded timidly.

"NEITHER THE MARBLE TOWER..."

Neither the marble tower in Pisa
Nor Niagara Falls
Nor the moon on a dark night
Nor a bare sword in its sheath of gold
Nor that alabaster pillar standing rigid
Can match the beautiful nakedness of this woman.

And no writing
Not the private words of a letter
Or the dazzling tongue of Solomon
Can be as sublime
As that one song issued
By the singer Drno
On a dreadful night.

END OF A STORY

In its own roundness
the girlish body shines
        and she opens her eyes,
to see more.
One's hand glides so easily
over the smooth skin.

Her head, too, is lovely and light
and it seems that her kiss cannot weigh more
than a fallen petal,
while the unattainable lips already hurry
to places that are jealously guarded
as if by both loin and doves.

A few years ago I was caught in a drunken wind,
and I did not heed these things.
        In one town,
a town that floats in the sea
like an ostrich-plumed hat,
a nun entered an empty church.

Almost as she entered,
she was devoutly on her knees.
A dove falls like that from the roof
        unto wet grass
when she wants to die.
Her forehead hidden under a veil moved
toward the colored air
as she uncovered her face.
God, I know this girl!

Perhaps it was a mistake and nothing more.

But I looked at her

as if bound to this memory.
She got up quickly, suffering on her face,
and before I could realize her shadow
the veiled appearance again disappeared
through the church's entrance
and faced the Guido fountains.

I rushed after her
to see one more time
her half-closed eyes,
in which lay
a wound
inflicted at the old well under the willow trees.

The black habit disappeared
among the lanes surrounding the Academy,
then I caught a glimpse of her far away
as she, now near the Palazzo Foscari,
walked on toward the Campo San Paolo.
I could see her white face
in the crowd at the fish market.
There I lost her forever—
as if she had hidden
among the silvery scales of fish.
Then the clock sang the songs
Written on the plastered walls of this city,
        struck ten—
Punctuations of time,
the roll of our blood.

"WHERE OR WHENEVER I HAD HEARD"

Where or whenever I had heard
Those country bells . . .

Their beating was gentle
And it seemed to me
They whispered kindly
Darling, Darling.

Then when they began ever so softly
With their tender chiming
I knew someone was crying,
Just like Bozheva Nemcova did,
With no one to hear her.

CROWNED WITH BERRIES

At the construction site, a heap of bricks
   The color of roses
And still hot as hands in fever,
Lay among children playing in the daytime.
In the evenings there,
Girls met their lovers.

One of them lived across the street.
And as darkness approached, following her
Was my curious need.
Even though she would sometimes
Turn on the sidewalks and stick her tongue
Out at me,
I could not leave her out of my sight.

My comrade told me all about
This older sister.
We hid in warm corners
Confiding in each other's secrets.
   That was intoxicating.

And once I had a whole wreath of fragrant berries,
Coveted much more than delicious honey
In cups with dusty covers
And which made you even dizzier
Than the liquid in the little skull-labeled
Bottle decorated with the word "poison"
That I always carried in my pocket.

But I am singing about a nonexistent bird.

I've got to smile.
Hush, place your ear to the door
And pay attention:
Love is lurking behind the door.

"WITH THE ROLL OF OUR BLOOD"

With the roll of our blood
    with the trample of fear
    with that spasm of passion
We suddenly step into the light
and dark desire puts our hand over the child's mouth.

Girls with crossed arms
protect their tender bodies
there where nature twice kissed them.
But the blood-crown
under one of those kisses
begins to grow slowly
and happiness, that first sunny one,
which we just now realize,
is almost over.

CANNON FIRE

When everyone kneels tomorrow
you will stand in white, festively,
because girls do not kneel when in white,
and you'll be as quiet
as a drop of water in my palm.
Only cannons will roar there
on the top of the hill, one after the other.

I saw you in the garden
    at the battle-field,
where twisted bowels stank
and puddles of blood stood full of green flies.

I picked a handful of flowers for you
but no one could weave as
beautiful a wreath as you.

Tomorrow the praying will begin,
those long prayers,
and I will smile at you over your splendid wreath.

I'm looking at your fingers,
lightly bending tight
around the jasmine bouquet,
and at the red rooster
with a fragrant mint leaf in his beak—
And the world begins swirling.
You look at me amazed,
and lift all the flowers
from your lap,
    drop everything on the floor—
I could have been convinced
that love up there in your heart
was just slumbering.

Everything is so sudden,
the aroused blood boils too soon,

Its wounds
    already the festive greeting
of a beauty
I had not yet recognized.

The devil, standing quite close,
surely a trigger-happy hunter,
saw my bewilderment and your shaking knees,
and viciously twisted his moustache.

"IN THOSE WINTERS WHEN..."

In those winters when the electricity died
And the broadcasts disappeared quietly over the
Luxurious disorder of everyday buckles and clasps and powder
I sat one morning by burning candle light
And listened to the music a comb played
With a woman's hair.

The flashing little sparks crackled silently,
Almost imperceptibly,
Brightening, again and again,
The world that was only dark before.

THE ARTISTS' HOUSE

I guarded leaves on the trees
snow on my windowsill
        and water in the faucet.
I'm already old like the lantern
on the Charles Bridge.
But sometimes I feel the threat.

Tomorrow
the shorthaired students of AMU will sit
on the steps in front of the Artists' House
—the Prague Spring begins
and the doors will open—
I'll gladly turn my eyes
and stare at the ground.

These young women are all one laughter,
suddenly pulling
their short skirts
a little over their knees—
They are so happy.

What would the author of fugue composition
        have said at this moment
in his silk coat
and silvery wig
as he hurried from the riverbank
to the main entrance!

Perhaps he can remember Magdalena,
but he surely did not see these girls.

And Mozart?

Mozart would have smiled,

and before going to his seat
he would have composed a dance.

"WHEN OUR MULBERRY TREES..."

When our mulberry trees bloom
Their smell often floats
Through my window . . .
Especially in the evening and after rain.

The trees are around the street corner,
    A couple of minutes away.
In the summertime, when I would run
Up to their hanging branches,
Noisy blackbirds had already picked
The dark fruit.

When I stand under those trees and breathe in
Their rich smell,
Life suddenly seems to collapse around me,
A strange luxurious feeling,
As if evoked by the touch
    of a woman's hand.

DANCE-SONG

It's been a long time since I wrote poems which dance—
And danced badly myself.
Still, sometimes even a stiff knee
Can beat good rhythm.

Now I go back shamefully
    To the first one:
She had tangled bronze hair which hung
In one thick braid down to the waist
And when she danced faster, and faster,
It flew heavily after her
Like a tamed bird.

And I often return to Jindrishka
    (Although I don't feel like it).
She vanished in the deep grass of this world
And I haven't seen her since.
But then
Just as my feet slide into my shoes
    I remember her
And the shoes take me to that face circled with ash blonde hair.

The third one, the one who always believed
That love was just loud kisses
And gentle words,
Is now angry with me.
The one under whose window I used to whistle
When she refused to show herself to me
    Danced superbly.
She always lost her little combs,
Broke her bracelet,
Her madonna's medal spilled to the floor,
And who knows what else.

But there isn't enough of anything as long as we live.

The feet suddenly stop,
The dance breaks up in the middle,
No need for strong arms until winter comes
And the palms of hands save themselves
For other work.

Finally, the last one appears.

She's confused, doesn't dance,
    That's why she's the most beautiful,
And is, until death, alone.

And now that one does not exist either.

"IF THE SAND COULD SING"

If the sand could sing
    under a woman's feet,
I would be one of those who believes
That a smile is near.
    And were it on the neck,
the light palm of a woman
would still have such strength
    that it could lift
any burden.
I'm sitting with a tired doctor-friend
in front of a pavilion.
    Little by little dusk descends.
These are the moments when there is talk
and people are listening
but no one hears anything.

We discuss women.
He is a gynecologist.
He starts laughing bitterly:
"Cynical soldiers in the Middle Ages
would not fight side-by-side with them
because they said that women were glum.
We can stand women only after fifty,
and even then it has to be done slyly.
    And love?
What can we say about that?
Damned genitals!"

And I got sick with yearning.
But that was not written
in my case history.

A REQUIEM FOR DVOŘÁK

Near Nelahozevse,
where sandstone cliffs boldly
hang out toward the Vltava river,
two lovers killed themselves.
They were young.
    It was a long time ago.
Today it could hardly happen.

One of those cliffs,
black from the smoke of locomotives,
looks like two human skulls.
In the smoke-filled eyes
wild doves build their nests.

The lovers jumped from the boat
        there, where the stream is darker.
Later the capsized boat was found
miles away at the shallow end.
All day long, people searched the river,
combing the narrow section.
Oh water, return us those bodies,
return them, you've had them long enough,
soon it will be evening.

For hours the hooked poles probed the depth,
touching, in vain, the rocky bottom.

It was dark when they were found.
They lay in the water in a lovely embrace,
bound by the cold mass.
At that moment everything froze still:
birds and wind,
        men's eyes, the stream.
And when they were pulled onto the boat,

the girl was completely naked.
The rocks on the bottom had taken off her clothes.
The men in the boat called to the shore:
    "Drag it out, boys!"
Well, you know, there were many of them.
But they did not move.
As if stuck to the ground in iced terror,
not one of them moved.

And now the fast train to Prague
ran its whistles through the mountains,
and everyone woke to the noise
and saw the emerging light fall
upon the wet legs of the girl,
broken at the knees.
Then someone swiftly covered her with
a blue jacket.
For heaven's sake,
    just tell me,
what kind of expression was hiding
in the eyes of those boys?

The excitement subsided
and a peaceful, normal day began.
The grass-pillows smelled hot
and invited lovers again
to the old game.

"IT'S AFTER ALL SAINTS DAY"

It's after All Saints Day,
the first snow falls
and a poet dies.
At the sound of bells
to which people run
whenever there is fire in the city,
the whole tower shakes.

Yet the bats sleep on.
Only birds perched on windowsills
fly out frightened,
but return to sit again after a moment
on top of the falling flakes.

Sometimes I remember
the grating of my pen,
with which I disgustedly scribbled
in the legal offices
of the attorney Duras in Litomerice.
Or the wedding ring
he wore a few days before the wedding.
Or that long sad letter
to the unhappy Lora
that so upset her and collapsed her life.
I have nothing.
All I have is a tiny volume
about love and May
which is frail and tender
like the breast
of a sixteen-year-old
who does not yet know
about that flower's beauty.

MYRTLE WREATH

In the Palace Street girls' school
a student died.
   She was thirteen
and all her schoolmates wept.
The dead live one more moment through those tears
and are then more beautiful than when they lived.

Although our school was next door,
we did not know the girl.
We had to walk away from the school entrance
on the other side of the street.
   That was an order.
Yet all of us went to the funeral
and I recognized her in the coffin.

I had seen her on the way to school.
Whenever I looked at her,
she started smiling a bit
   just through the handle of her bag.
Good-bye. It was drizzling.

When it rains, the earth becomes heavier.
Yet she soon returned,
Quietly knocking on my door
   like the thread on a loom
and came in always in the evening,
when I was hiding under my blanket
and tried to sleep.
Her lips a trifle open,
she smiled a little
   and sat at my bed.
The rest was told by her eyes
ever so quietly.
A streetcar noisily rolled by under my window.

At night I dreamed
that I met her again
as I was running to school one morning.

Thus she came three, four times,
    even five times
but I could see her only in shadow,
as if in the light of a used flash
when the wire in the bulb is getting just pink.
I could still see her face,
her sad eyes,
and the chair became empty.

And across that chair I found
only my miserable pants.

"ARE YOUR POEMS YOUR SONGS..."

Are your poems your songs as well?
I have been singing all my life
And sided with those who had nothing
And lived from hand to mouth.
I was one of them.

I sang their sorrows,
        their faith and hope,
And I lived with them just
As they lived: the anxiety,
Weakness, fear, even courage,
And, always the sadness of misery.
Their blood, when it flowed,
Stained my face, branded me.

Too much of it was spent
On this earth of sweet rivers, long grass,
        and delicate birds.

And I sang about women also.
Blinded by their love
        I roamed in life
Burying withered flowers
On the steps of a cathedral.

MY STAR-HUNG WINDOW

In those summers, when I quickly
licked off the currant jam from my bread,
        I believed
that there couldn't be more stars in the sky
than the white points
on my mother's apron.

Lately I've been sitting
by the window under the arched roof
and have watched the well-known star groups
and invented brand new ones myself:
one of the Coral branch,
and at its beginning
        the group of the Turkish saber,
then the Ring group,
then Cinderella's slipper,
the Fiddle stars
in the fog of silver webs.

When someone opened my door,
a fuse of streaking lights
spread over the floor.

And once I saw
        five shining stars,
and remembered Andromeda,
naming them after our pretty teacher,
whom I secretly loved.

Her name was Marie Kolarova.
I saw her once at Sophia Beach.
She swam backstroke in the river.
The first two stars were her eyes.
And she let herself be carried by the stream
toward Strelecky Island.

WHEN WE ARE DENIED

When we are denied,
to recall
our mother's warm blood,
again and again we can return
but to our childhood,
to that short-lived bliss,
which seems already to be the last joy
in our life.

At the mercy of life,
we are making but one big detour
from the first hurt.
Our eyes see light only once
until that moment when someone
covers them with a cloth
and a merciful darkness
envelops us again.

HEAVENLY BONDS

Some seconds before her death
our mother turned her face toward us
and hoarsely said:
    "There is nothing."
Then her lips quietly closed forever.

To what unfathomable pit fell
        her rose wreath
kiss-covered a hundred times,
where did all those prayers fall
and the whispered songs,
that she used to sing when she was a girl?
Where did fear and anxiety go
from all the petty deeds?
The names of all sins are defined clearly
and are right or wrong
        and the right ones are just as good
as the rest.

What kind of darkness did she experience
        in that one short second,
when our feet spring off the earth,
just to fall back on it again?

I went out to the balcony quietly
and from my mother's shabby chair
I looked up somewhere
toward the stark heights.
For all our long life
they gape at us in the window,
not demanding anything.
Not wanting anything from us,
        and if you will,
they're indescribably beautiful.

And we try to wipe them out
with ivy seeds,
        rose seeds,
words and tears!

And finally we want to tear open
        their shining locks
with our last breath,
which is, even in our powerful throats,
the weakest.

"NOT TOO LONG AGO . . ."

Not too long ago I read in the news
that somewhere they're about to order
the bells to be quiet.
They will lower the decibels
in the bustling pandemonium of the city.
The bells are at fault.
    Let them shut up.

Besides, if there were no bells in the steeples,
there would be enough metal
        for bullets and grenades.
Cannons would have something to do,
more time for war.

Mrs. Lactitia Dytrychova,
the last one of those
who can cast bells,
could lay her hands in her lap.
But what about the poets?
    They're possessed with the idea
that bells keep being heard in that great sound.
There are certain moments when they write
that darkness is reversed,
midnight jumps back,
        the clocks stop striking,
the teeth quietly chatter
and storm transforms one's hair into a whirl.

Tell me, what would happen to those poets,
who want to be there
until under the blows of civilization
the world's threads start flying around in shreds
and the white smocks of scientists, so carefully stitched,
fall open?

Poets want at all costs
to cry out their verses.
Still, the one I'm whispering to you,
is only a couple of quiet words.
    No more.
And the words will meet your eyes.

MONUMENT TO A KETTLE DRUM

When you hurt somewhere,
a glass of wine
and a friendly hand
work better for your spirit
than medicine, bandages, or even Peruvian balsam.
Some time ago in the late afternoon
I knocked at the atelier door
    of the sculptor Karl Dvořák.

"Sit down and pour yourself one,
    I'll be ready in a minute."
And he quietly worked
on a nude.

The spatula was sliding on the wet clay
from the big knot of hair downward
like a tiny rivulet between the heaps,
where peaceful light falls, toward
the flat of the back
which is separated by a girdle,
and was pulled across the belly
to a lovely tumult.
The sculptor touched his finger
to the wet clay here and there
ever so lightly, as if it were somehow burning.
And, in the end, he enveloped everything with his eyes.
I poured myself three glasses.
The third one for the model
who was still getting dressed behind a panel
over which a stained raincoat
was thrown, interrupting the small flat surface.

When this man worked on a monument
for the Svatovitsky Cathedral,

he was already seriously crippled.
But the less life remained in him,
the more he hurried stubbornly
to finish shaping in stone.

Even the noise of the streets
could not still
the sculptor's chisel three blocks away,
until it set down the notes of a kettle drum.
But the intervals between
the hyperite injections
ominously shortened.
From months to weeks,
from weeks to days.
And when I noticed that he worked
behind the door just ajar,
I didn't even stop in.

We know no one can avoid death,
but Dvořák has proven with his broad gesture
that man must not stand before her
desperately defenseless.
It *is* possible to express
        one's defiance
and death will be subdued.
That is the only answer.

I LOOKED ONLY

I looked only once
at the sun so blood-red.
    And then never again.

As I slowly approached my window
it happened:
Someone pushed in Hell's gate.

I asked at the Observatory
and now I know why.

We are told that Hell is everywhere
and walks by twos.
    But Paradise?
Maybe Paradise is nothing more
than that laugh
    we have been waiting for so long,
and its mouth is the one
    that whispers our name.

But, of course, when it happens,
in that short, fragile moment
we will dare to remember
Hell.

ORANGEADE

At the surrealists' exhibit in Paris
they were selling female breasts
made from soft elastic rubber.
  I don't know why, nor do I know the cup sizes.
They were real!
  All nightingales, strutting feather and flute,
sing the same melody.
  The old hard-working fishermen
  Used to say: Something's wrong with him,
Something's definitely wrong with him.

That was a happy, carefree time
and I've already forgotten the last digit of the year.
The Sacre Coeur was floating quietly in a spring storm
like a big whale . . .
a shimmering tower of fountain,
and war was far away from this place,
  keeping its battles for another time.

I was breakfasting at a cafe under the canvas
at the Boulevard Montparnasse
and a black woman, smiling,
sat down next to my little table:
a thin, white, knitted sweater covered her bare body.
She was drowsy, a little sleepy in the warm morning
and her flesh looked like the deep center
of a honeycomb, where the nectar is dark.
At home, when our maples bloom,
their honey is a lighter gold.
Our mind forces our hands to remain
still in such mornings, not to touch.
But what about our eyes?

The sky was blue.
  Paris smiled,

and I listened as a piece of ice
clinked against her teeth.
And as she emptied her glass,
        as the ice fell abruptly to the bottom
she put two fingers to her wet lips,
lightly kissed them,
and quickly pressed them to my forehead.

She got up at once and ran to the Metro entrance,
where the train was sounding its horn.
In that morning air, her palm was the light pink
of wild hedge roses.
Yes, wild roses, somewhere at home
blooming over a small stone fence in early June.

This is what happened at the little cafe, under the canvas,
on the Boulevard Montparnasse.

"BEFORE THOSE FEW LIGHT KISSES..."

Before those few light kisses dry up
on your forehead
you're bending down to drink
from crystal clear water,
and no one doubts
whether you touched the lips of their mouth.

There are moments when,
faster than running fingers
on sculptor's clay,
impatient blood models
your body from the inside.

Perhaps you will put her
young hair in your palms
and lift it over her shoulder
to resemble two stretched wings,
and run after them heavily
there,
        where right before your eyes
and deep below the air
is that steep, terrifying
and sweet nothing,
        that sparkles.

THE MOUNT OF VENUS

Oh, yes, innocent lovemaking!
　　　But as a good friend said,
not even love could do
without a little blissful sinning.
Only that will excite and warm
and chase away monotony.
But love doesn't have to put on
the colors of bleached-out pants
and tight overalls.

Besides, you seldom find out
what women are really thinking about.
Their little thoughts elude you
just as small birds barely touch the human voice
when their claws clench the phone lines.

But women, even with half-shut eyes,
read with passion
　　　what's written on lips
that are definitely closed.
What a great mystery this is on our earth!

Our world is shameless
because we have divided it.
　　　And when was it any better?
We're erring day after day, aimlessly,
Yet long for the future.

But tomorrow has already been here,
　　　and we've missed it.
We constantly go in circles
while despair and sorrow
harass our minds.

Up until today we could hear the thunder of wars

that mercilessly paved the dark road to peace
with human bones.

But we prefer to think of women.
        Those zippers,
just how long can they surround themselves
with dim and bright lights,
and when they put a belt around
their full round tenderness,
our mind races in its own vanity.

And they're so glad to smile
even when they, at candlelight, listen in the evening
to the nostalgic vespers.
Even hope has that ridiculousness about it
and man, as you may well know, can, after all endure anything.
Even death!
        By then, it's already still and quiet.

"YOU ARE ASKING, . . ."

You are asking, what more can women accomplish?
Evidently everything.

Place three pieces of straw
across a precipice,
They'll walk over with a light foot.
How? I can't explain these things.
But remember
it was they who invented the dance.

In their easy moments
they will go to the Black Forest
to dig up ferns.
And if they linger until night
they will boldly place the morning candles
on the pathway so that the lonely traveler who comes
will not fear the dark morass.

Even the shy flowers are advised
to fill their chalices
with authentic scent.
They'll prove how to deal with accents,
        sword in hand,
much more dangerous
than the scorpion's poison.

Oh, the female breast
is the Chateau of Loire,
but more beautiful,
and their children suckling
to the passionate lullabies
are born to the songs that come
from their brief sleep in the castle.

Still, when women want to fall in love,

they tie their webs around someone,
(often in the heat of Indian summer).
They tie him so securely
that his blood will pour
and they create such a
profound depression in their love
that you too will be drowned.
I won't even mention it all.
Masked passions control their caresses,
silently crying to lull evil thoughts to sleep;
yet they wake the sleeping man again with their kisses.
(But that is delight!)
They will draw the curtains together
with just one breath,
easily pulling it up and letting it fall again,
because, right then (as we watch from across the street)
they are taking their clothes off,
just to cover later, at will,
their nakedness.
And not even the gala dresses of Dior
sewn with golden spangles
can match that.

But what do men accomplish?
Not much of anything.
They invented war,
misery, despair and the cry of the wounded.
They can foment vain ideas,
turn cities to rubble
and thereby exhibit
stinking male bravery.

They invented gas pumps
and equal rights for women.

And for kisses and embraces
they built special seats
to enable the sewing wife
to work more
during the last month of her pregnancy.

This is how it is.
And that is all, good-bye, adieu.
You wanted a cantilena from me,
there you are!

A LETTER FROM MARIENBAD

On Sunday morning,
When the colonnade is liveliest,
And the old trees
With their regal crowns
Quiver in solitude,
The nearby church bells ring
And the resort band begins
Its usual Viennese waltz:
    It is like the scene
    Of an aging husband
    Confessing ardent love to his wife
    While she sits typing a letter to her lover.

Listen: My days go by quickly
    Yours never do.
Age is a cheerless walk
By empty gardens in November
When it's dark and raining.

Have you seen the lilies blooming?

Our peacock, after walking all day,
Will sit on a branch in the eve
And spread out like a canopy.

Stop this sleeping! Wake up!

It may be that in this life
Even the last sad event,
The inevitable end,
Doesn't mean anything.
The poppies we find in the sack
Of white grain disappear
In the bottomless one, the black one,
The one that is always empty.

But before the band starts playing
We will go for an ice-cream.
I'll walk beside you trailing smoke
From my pipe and then watch you
Tenderly select the black cone.

No, do not think that someone else
Will spoil my good mood:
Even those who look above their heads
Only at night
Blow at least one breath against the window pane—
Their name now in wet dust—something remains.

Last night, thinking about you,
I wanted to write to your eyes.
Perhaps then you'd look once at me
Whenever you'd glance on dim walls,
Where everything is hidden, at your feet
On the sidewalk, or in the evening,
As your eyes slowly close,
Or next morning when the birds announce loudly
That the night is undressing
And then grow silent when she leaves, naked.

Blood, soil, love, freedom, power
Are all your eagle-children dear—
Like death itself:
And there is no escape from these embraces.

Even the waterfall caresses the rocks
With a lovely woman's beauty.
Everything, a tuft of grass
And the flags waving,
The soft spot in the nest,

The moist chalice of a pompous flower
Reminds us of you.

To this day men are being menaced
By ruthless beauty,
As they were in that age when people
Were mercilessly chaste
Yet still had the courage to love.
Even though the hours change, it is a common history;
And the colonnade is the epoch of rose.

I know well enough what you're about to say.

Hold me long in your entanglement,
        A woman's laces,
The rose withering in the poet's lines.
Still it is the blossom of love that moves us,
The language opening flowers reveal,
And until bosoms break the bars of whale bones
A new era will not begin.
But today we are already distant from those times,
We are close, close—close to what?
Close to that which we do not know!
And unhappy, miserable, cast off the throne.

There was a time when artists placed
The tools of laughter and complaint
In carefully made boxes—
But suddenly the colonnade looks so tall.
And over the tops of the rigid pinnacles
We see the sky . . .

Have you seen the lilies blooming?
Their sources run deep,

Spreading among the roots,
Their sound is full of pure silver.

Now someone pulls at my sleeve
And I awake to a face
That is familiar:
When I was young
I always believed you hid from me
Behind the trees.
None of those I have met since were like you.

And as if I were casually unwinding
A soft yarn of wool for her, she said quietly:
"You know I am very much alone
        and always the same."
        Those . . . were my kisses.

Why then do you come so late?
I was just strapping tight my empty luggage,
        Getting ready to leave
To where the little flames of blown-out candles
Fly noiselessly.

To that she whispered:
"Don't rush. Over the long course
Everything but hope will let you go,
Even I will let you go—and I am you."

Then come away with me now.
Even if I lose you again, it is
As intangible as time,
Your steps, as if you had walked in blood,
Will trail after me a little while at least.
She smiled and grew silent.

I don't know who chose this,
Of all lands, for my puzzlement.
No, in fact, I do know.
I often thought about that circumstance:
For me, there is nothing more beautiful
In this world than chance.

Remember when I first brushed off
        The rain that covered you
And, in my anxiety, could barely look at you.
I put my face close to your hair
        And held my breath a minute.
Then I could take a deeper breath
And hurl a thousand kisses to your eyes
        And see them close and blinding.

It is that smiling game
In which men whisper their passions—
        Wait a little longer—
And women seem reluctant
For those few seconds as they play.
Then the man asks the woman:
"Tell me, what am I thinking about?"
She will guess immediately;
The rest is up to fate.
The man goes near,
        So he can touch the naked tree,
Only wanting to be held, loved,
And overcome.

But love, and war, bring us to churches—
To men and crowds,
        And blood, that passionate flag
Waving at our foreheads as always.

Even when we go to die.

So death and love have been here before.
Even spring returns each year always the same.
Why reproach her for it?

Have you seen the lilies bloom?
Among the slender stems
        The small blue ones shine—
And those are your eyes
Watching from behind frail fingers,
        With laughter choking your palms.

Laugh at me,
        I'm to be laughed at, I know,
And hide, as if you knew only that about me.
As long as I can grasp for air,
I will faithfully crawl after you.
And when I capture you, you'll be mine only.
You are as real as a blade of grass,
And more so than the sky.
        I'm clutching your tender wrists
As if I were holding on to the burning bars of Hell.
        But there is no hell.
                It is only you.
Even the sky is mere semblance,
And I just invented the grass blade,
        And now even you do not exist.

There is only the black, cold emptiness
Which we are approaching.

But still we hold tenaciously
To our passionate life.

I still feel your cold forehead
  Leaning toward me.
I still taste the sweet water of your lips,
  The heat of your blood—
I still feel your crystal teeth against my fingers.

Surely in our lives
We have nothing but our own bodies.
Sometimes it is just too difficult.
But it is the end of all ends,
Our only possession.

All the rest is trouble-filled preludes
And a twinkle in the shadows.